THE SELECTION OF PICTURES IN THIS BOOK BROUGHT
BACK A LOT OF MEMORIES FOR THE BAND. IT WAS
FASCINATING TO SEE OURSELVES FROM 1963 TO 1971.
IT CERTAINLY PROVIDES A GOOD PICTORIAL
BIOGRAPHY OF OUR EARLY YEARS.

WE WOULD ALL LIKE TO WISH THE BOOK EVERY
SUCCESS AND HOPE IT ALSO BRINGS BACK SOME
HAPPY MEMORIES FOR THOSE WHO READ IT.

MICK JAGGER

THE ROLLING STONES

DEZO HOFFMANN WITH NORMAN JOPLING

THE ROLLING STONES

DEZo HOFFMAN

Born in Czechoslovakia, Dezo Hoffmann began his long career behind the camera in Prague as clapper-boy on the Hedi Lamarr movie *Eroticon*. As newsreel cameraman for 20th Century Fox, he covered Mussolini's invasion of Abyssinia, and later – while he was in Barcelona for the Olympiad Popular (the alternative 1936 Olympics) – 'the civil war broke out in front of my eyes'. He stayed to cover the war, becoming the accredited correspondent of the Republican side, and was subsequently seriously wounded. At the outset of the Second World War Dezo joined the Czech army, eventually arriving in England in 1940. The War Office quickly utilized his experience, sending him as a newsreel cameraman to all major theatres of war.

After the war he joined the Crown film unit, but soon found more excitement and creative potential in press photography. He specialized in show-biz celebrities – Charlie Chaplin, Louis Armstrong, Marilyn Monroe, Frank Sinatra, Marlene Dietrich – and was amongst the first to use colour film for this work. His coverage of the London music and entertainment scene remains unrivalled; his pictures of the Beatles, Cliff Richard and the Shadows, and the Rolling Stones have become standard reference material.

During a lifetime of photography Dezo Hoffmann has built up a library of over a million negatives and many of his pictures have become archetypal images. He continues to work internationally.

INTRODUCTION

This is essentially one photographer's experience of the Rolling Stones. The images in this collection were conceived strictly as news pictures – to be seen today and forgotten tomorrow. Dezo Hoffmann had no pretensions towards art photography, and no eye towards any future collections of his work. It is, therefore, an even greater tribute to his skills that his pictures are now being recognized as some of the finest and most evocative of their time.

The photographs in this book were taken mostly in the 1960s when the Rolling Stones were based in London. Dezo was then the staff photographer for *Record Mirror*, the first music paper to feature the group, and these pictures chronicle them during their early years of success.

Dezo's approach to still photography was unique in that he almost always used available light in preference to flash – this was a technique learned from years as a film-maker. It gives the photographs an uncommon depth and substance, and many of the studies here – particularly the portraits – are amongst the best of the Stones from this period.

This was a *Record Mirror* assignment and they sent along their R & B expert Norman Jopling to see what all the fuss was about. He didn't believe a British group could play R & B; after seeing them he wrote a fantastically enthusiastic report. The day it appeared in *Record Mirror* three major record companies phoned him to ask where they could contact the Stones.

These were the days when Ian Stewart (top right) was still in the Stones. He played piano and maracas, and drove the van. When Andrew Loog Oldham took over as manager, Ian was relegated to road manager. He's still working for the group . . . .

They were called the Rollin' Stones then, so the other big change Andrew made was to alter their name slightly.

A Variety Club of Great Britain venue – the Stones' first big outdoor concert in London. Decca had signed them and their reputation was growing all the time. There was a whole array of stage and film stars there, but the Stones were one of the biggest attractions.

Their first professional photographic
session. All the groups at the time wore
uniforms, but the Stones' were a bit more
casual than most. The leather waistcoats
were Andrew's idea, but the boys didn't
wear them very much afterwards. When I
began the session, Brian didn't have any
cuff links, so I lent him mine – they were
gold, a wedding present from my wife. I
never got them back and later I heard that
Brian had given a pair of gold cufflinks
to Bo Diddley around that time. The
Stones' first tour was with the Everly
Brothers, Little Richard, and their hero,
Bo Diddley.

Brian Poole and the Tremeloes were
booked in for the photo session after the
Stones. They arrived early, so I introduced
the two groups and asked them to pose
together. Brian Poole was hesitant about
having his picture taken with an almost
unknown group, because at that time he
was one of the biggest acts in the country.
I wanted the picture partly because they
were both Decca artists. You can see I put
the two leaders, the two Brians, together
at the front. Funny . . . but they didn't stay
the leaders for very long.

They had found marvellous offices in a modern building right opposite Regent's Park, very near the private residence of the American ambassador. There was no furniture though, and I tried to capture that atmosphere . . . it was fifties tatty when they moved in; the old wallpaper looked like marijuana plants!

Rediffusion Television had leased a building in Kingsway, London, and allocated the basement to producer Elkan Allen for 'Ready Steady Go!' It was quite a shell and no one at the time really knew what they were doing – this show was a new kind of thing. When you look at the pictures from 'RSG' over the years, you can see how much the studio improved.

Their new record was 'I Wanna Be Your Man', which the Beatles had written for them. When Andrew saw how quickly John and Paul wrote it, he encouraged Keith and Mick to write together, although they didn't really want to. They even said to Norman Jopling, 'Can you imagine a British-composed R & B number – it just wouldn't make it.' But Andrew had seen how much money the Beatles were making from their own songs, and he was the one who really started off the Jagger-Richards songwriting team. Andrew himself had graduated from being a runner-boy for one of the Tin Pan Alley music companies, and was just about to see his ship come in.

Here they are waiting to go on . . . this part of the basement later became known as Reception.

The 'Ready Steady Go!' studio was already taking shape by this time – you can see even the cameras are marked RSG. The boys are singing 'Not Fade Away'.

Cathy McGowan interviewing Mick. She was one of the programme's presenters and was always very fashionable. When I took this shot, I had to use a special muffler on my camera so that the click would not be heard on her microphone.

Pre-rehearsal conversation between Tony Calder (left), who was Andrew's right-hand man, Mick's brother, Chris (centre), and Billy J. Kramer (at any rate, the back of his head).

The first Rolling Stones window-display promotion by Decca. It was in Alex Strickland's Soho Record Centre on the corner of Dean Street and Old Compton Street. I couldn't do a picture during the day because it was always so crowded – I had to wait and do it one evening. Note the other record sleeves on display: 'The Freewheeling Bob Dylan', 'Session' by the Dave Clark Five, 'A Girl Called Dusty', amongst others.

The Stones were very big in Europe, and this session was taken when they flew off for a tour which took in Germany and Scandinavia. They were getting a big fan following here, second only to the Beatles, and the police were now needed to hold back the fans. Here they are posing on the tarmac. Brian was still considered the leader, but the spotlight was already focusing more and more on Mick.

They gave interviews to newsreel and press reporters in the VIP lounge. You can see the cine cameras at the back. Andrew Loog Oldham is wearing the dark glasses, and next to him is Ian Stewart, the demoted Rollin' Stone who accepted his fate gracefully.

MAD MOD BALL

The Stones were one of the few British groups that appealed to the mods, but by this time the mod movement had really just become a commercial craze. Here are Mick and Charlie backstage with Wee Willie Harris, who was one of the great colourful characters of British rock-'n'-roll. He was almost pre-pre-punk, a real innovator. Willie looks very smart here: in the past he would dye his hair pink and wear animal-skin costumes.

ON THE AIR

The BBC hired the Albert Hall once a week for their Light Programme 'Top Beat' live show – this was the beginning of live pop broadcasting. It had tremendous listening figures, and captured the whole country and beyond. Everybody who was somebody did this show at one time or another. The picture is a rehearsal shot.

Andrew Loog Oldham held a general photo-call in the park and to show off his new offices. Everybody in the park seemed to ask for autographs and the Stones willingly signed hundreds of them.

They didn't want to sit down because the grass was wet, but eventually they put down their dirty handkerchiefs and sat on them. Here I am, the photographer on the right, while Andrew is making horrible faces to get the boys to smile. My assistant took this picture – the other picture (inset) is one I was taking of the group at the time.

The office and Andrew's own flat were on the seventh floor and by this time had been completely refurbished. Here he is pretending to be terribly busy on the phones – two Coke bottles. Actually, all the telephones were connected, but on that day none of them was ringing, because nobody knew the new phone number.

You can see how much the 'RSG' studio has improved. DJ Keith Fordyce was another of the programme's presenters; here he is interviewing Bill. The boys' hit record at that time was 'It's All Over Now'.

Mick and Charlie were in a quandry here, discussing the order in which to perform their songs. Brian had decided the order earlier, but the others disagreed.

Brian wanted the group to be on a different side of the studio because he felt it had a nicer background, and here he is showing Keith Fordyce where he wants them to be. But Keith was only the linkman and Brian didn't realise he should have been talking to the show's floor-manager. In the end they stayed where they were.

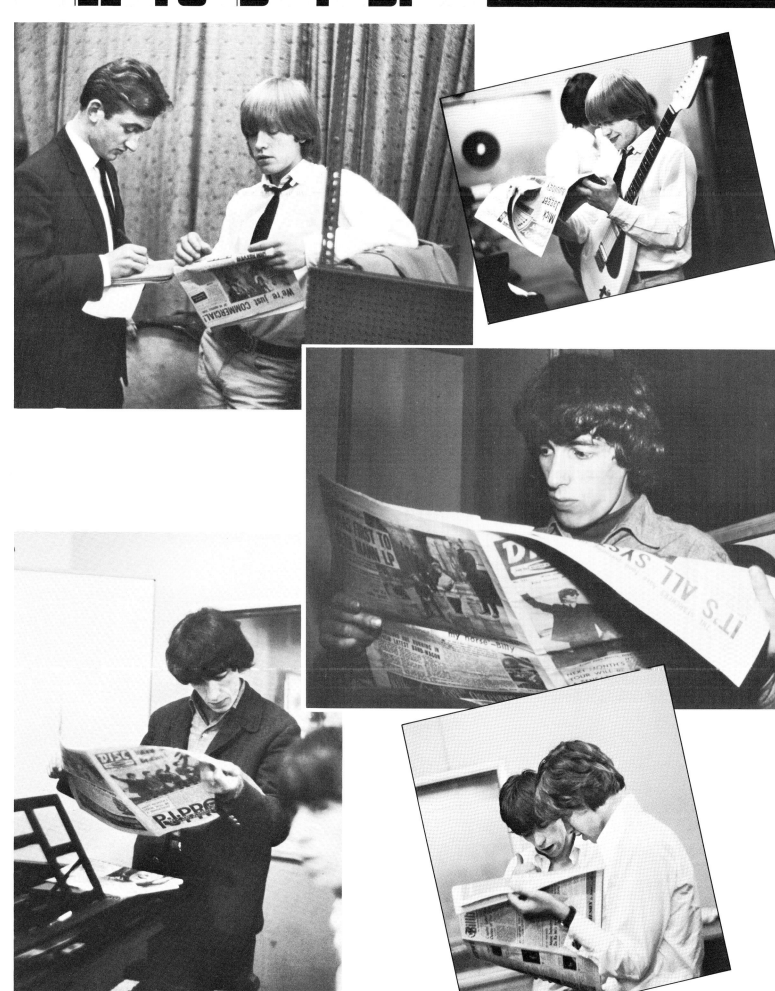

recording session
here some of the press
rned up. Keith Altham of
e *New Musical Express*
interviewing Brian –
later became a very
ccessful publicist,
king over the Stones' PR
ter the death of Leslie
errin. Mick and Keith are
oking in the *Billboard*
harts to see if their
cords are doing
ything in America.
heir first tour there the
onth before had been a
isaster.

This was 'RSG's first anniversary programme and featured many big stars, including Gerry, Cilla, Billy J. Kramer, Paul McCartney, the Nashville Teens, Brian Poole and the Trems, and Marianne Faithful. She was then having a big hit with Mick and Keith's song 'As Tears Go By'.

Brian entering the main studio, flanked by 'RSG' technicians.

RICHMOND JAZZ FESTIVAL

The Fourth National Jazz Festival was organized by Harold Pendleton's National Jazz Federation, and the Stones went back to play at the old Crawdaddy Club for the first time in a year. There were seven thousand fans at the festival. The MC was Giorgio Gomelsky, who had been the Stones' manager before Andrew and Eric Easton took over. Giorgio's new group, the Yardbirds, also played, but the Stones were the big attraction. Today, Giorgio is working successfully in New York.

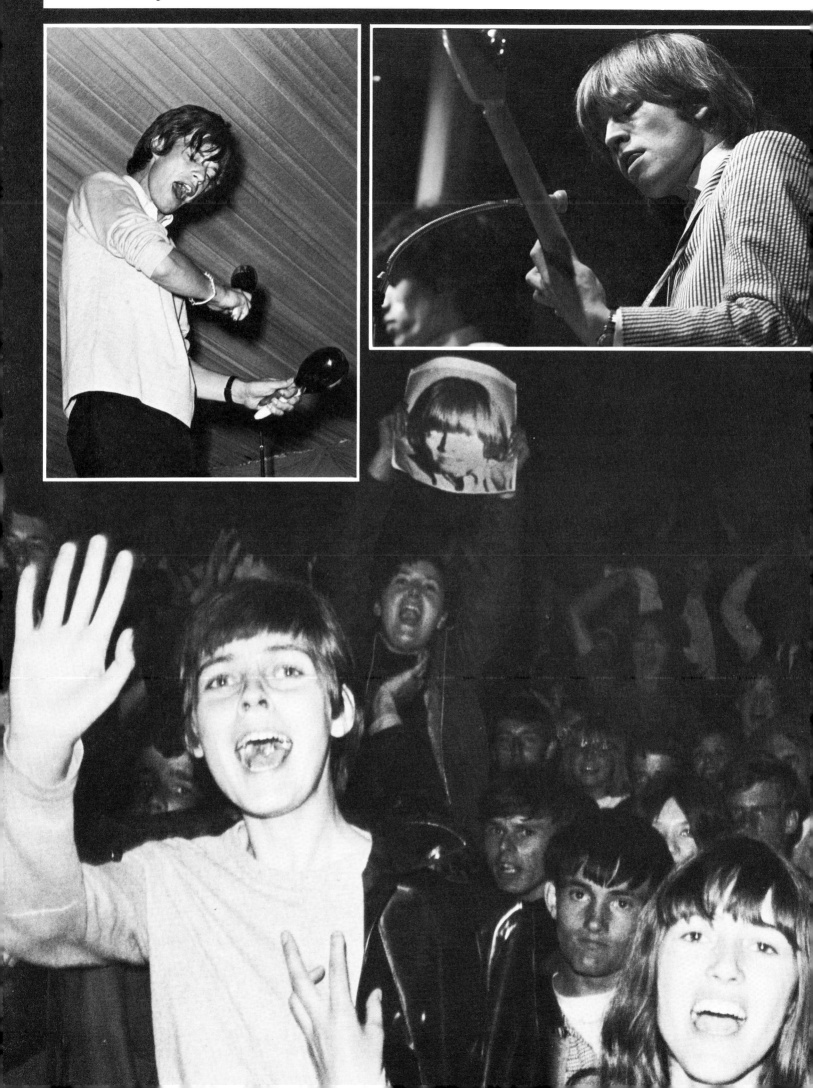

This was a Variety Club of Great Britain dinner held at the Savoy Hotel, and the photos were taken in the foyer. Mick is with Sir Joseph Lockwood, chairman of EMI. I thought it would make a nice picture because EMI were the big rivals of Decca, who recorded the Stones. I asked Sir Joseph if he wouldn't mind, and he agreed. Many years later the Stones actually did sign for EMI.

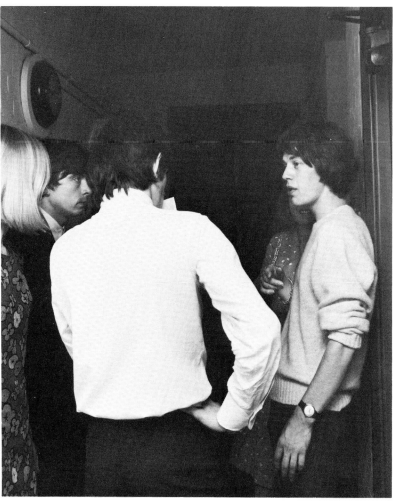

Mick and Keith (with his back to the camera) are talking with David Bailey (left). Bailey took the cover picture of their first album. It was the first time in Britain that the name of the artist was not on the front of the sleeve.

Their first major appearance in Britain after they had become big stars. They had also made it in America by this time.

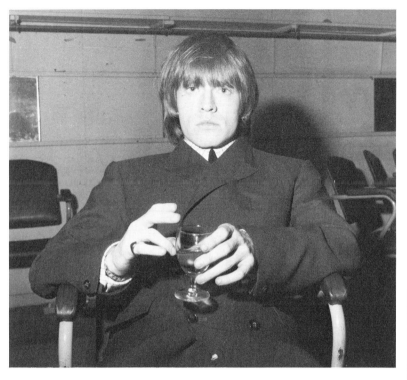

Keith and Humphrey Lyttleton, Britain's leading traditional jazzman.

These girls pulled the floats, trying to clear a path through the debris. You can see the mops with the boys' names on them.

Mick poses by camera 2 in the 'RSG' studio.

Brian was giving an interview for Radio
Luxembourg at their studios in Hertford
Street where he met Donovan, who was
then touted as Britain's answer to
Bob Dylan. Although they each had
separate interviews, I took this picture of
them together with songwriter and
money-maker Geoff Stephens.

1964 had been a great year for the Stones. Here at Decca's annual Christmas binge 'Avengers' heroine Honor Blackman is with Mick and Decca executive Marcel Stellmann.

Andrew's new protégé, Cleo, hangs onto a merry Brian.

I wanted just Alan Freeman with the Stones, but everybody else wanted to be in the picture.

Mick is wearing his enigmatic Mona Lisa smile. He is actually quite mesmerized and flabbergasted at the spectacle of Tom Jones, Kenny Lynch and the Animals pillow-fighting in a big bed set up in the 'RSG' studio. Mick decided not to join the undignified Christmas prank. Keith, also thoughtful, was obviously in the same serious frame of mind as Mick. He too looked at the pillow-fight with mild disapproval. The Rolling Stones were not always wild!

The boys triumphant after a successful take. Mick's mock Heil Hitler salute did not go unnoticed, especially as the Stones were by now the bad boys of pop. Andrew had masterminded this, realizing that as the Establishment embraced the Beatles closer and closer, youngsters needed a more rebellious group with which to identify.

A whole battalion of secondary-school girls turned up at this particular show, which was a sort of Stones special. Mick is talking to the girls' teacher.

Their new record was
'The Last Time', and
Mick and Cathy are
discussing how best
to introduce it.

Two of the schoolgirls with a crush on
Keith decided to write his name in
lipstick on each other's cheeks.

Brian and Bill checking to see if
their instruments are in tune.
They always took a long time
tuning up in those days.

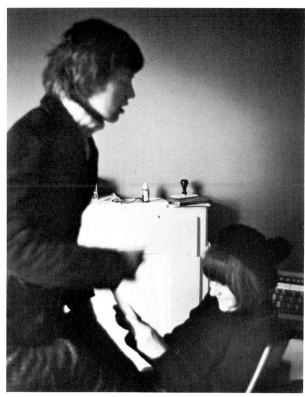

This session was taken in and around their West End offices. Here's Mick with Chrissie Shrimpton, his first much-publicized girlfriend, who was the sister of top model Jean Shrimpton. Some of the boys are going through an enormous batch of fan mail, and Mick and Keith are on the piano, tinkling together on a one-finger exercise, possibly working it up into a top-line tune. They also wrote songs as Nanker-Phelge in those days. Afterwards I dragged them out into the street and took the group shots.

A press reception held at a recording studio. You can see the rather primitive equipment and also glimpse Keith making a very strong point about something to Andrew. They're drinking Coke and beer from *cans*, which were quite a novelty then.

The Stones had recorded the Drifters' hit 'Under The Boardwalk' at Chess studios in Chicago the year before, and Brian met the legendary American vocal group at a Decca press reception in Gt Marlborough Street, London. The line-up (left to right) is Johnny Moore (lead singer), Charles Thomas, Brian, Johnny Terry and Eugene Pearson.

'READY – TEADY G...!'

Andrew Loo
Oldham is tryir
to clear up a fe
technical points wi
'RSG' produce
Elkan Allen, whi
Brian and Kei
appear to be lookir
for the lost chor
and finding it at la:

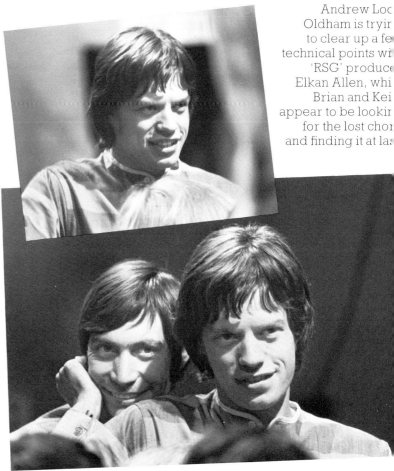

MICK TAYLOR'S FLAT

Brian left the Rolling Stones under a great cloud of secrecy and was replaced in June 1969 by Mick Taylor, a very good guitarist who had been playing blues with John Mayall. In the beginning the new Mick felt a little out of his depth, but he soon found his feet and adjusted to instant fame.

Mick Taylor relaxing in his flat, a man with something to smile about.

They were setting up
the free concert in
Hyde Park and this was
a photo-call for the
press to see the new
line-up with Mick
Taylor. They were also
checking the general
layout for the concert,
planned for July.

This was their first concert for two years. It was held just a few days after Brian died.

For me, the concert marked a change in the youth, the end of Swinging London, the point when it all started to decline. It was nothing to do with the Stones, but I think this was when it all began to go downhill. It was here that the kids, the audience, began acting up for the media, everyone wanting to get in on the act. You could also see it from the way Carnaby Street was going.

Keith interviewed for *Record Mirror*.

LYCEUM THEATRE DECEMBER 1969

The Stones had just come back from America and although they were still very shocked about Altamont, they put on a terrific Christmas show. Half a mile of fans queued along the Strand, but there was no trouble. Inside the theatre the fans were covered with artificial snow from a huge bag hung on the ceiling. Mick looked really spectacular and was in amazing form vocally.

T E ROLLI G ~T E ~'OFFI E

This was a farewell party for Shirley Arnold, who had run the Rolling Stones' office for a long time. It was quite a hectic occasion, with people like Elton John and Ronnie Lane dropping in, but it was still quite homely. At that time their offices were in New Oxford Street, but later these offices were taken over by Dick James Music.

The two Micks talking together.

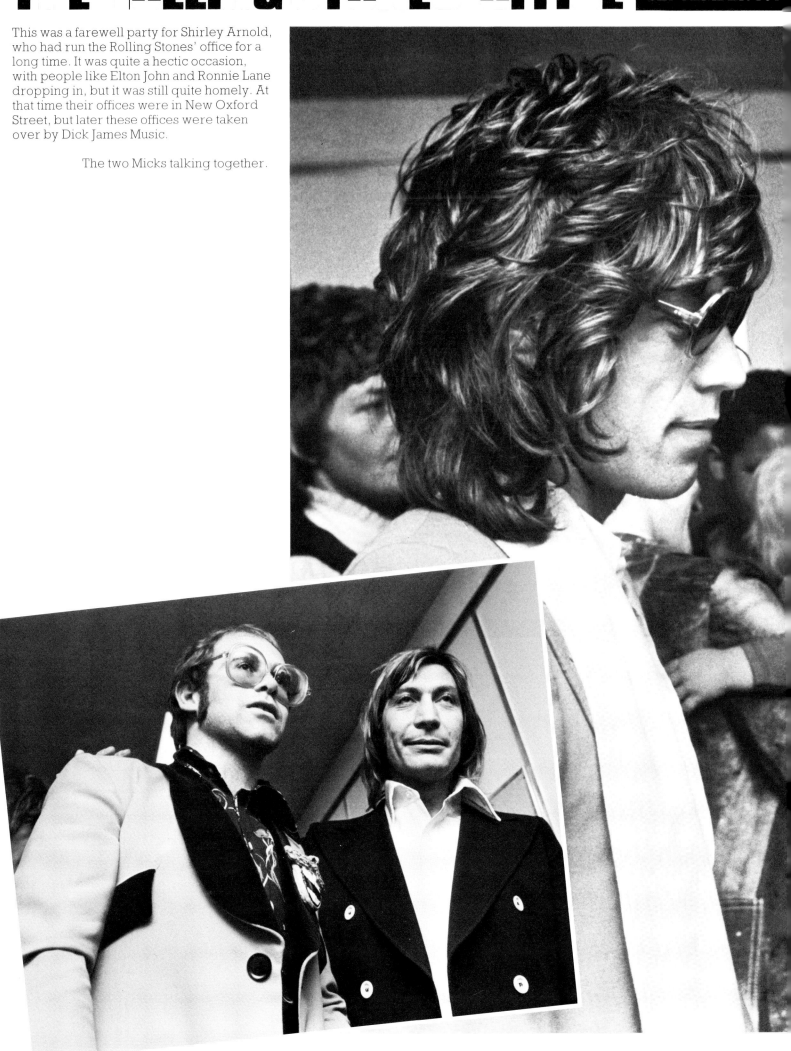

Mick went into a private office to make a call
to his wife, Bianca, who arrived later on.

Mick with Shirley Arnold.

There were lots of laughs. Leslie Perrin (left) is also enjoying the joke.

Charlie with Chris Jagger.

Billy Gaff of GM Records threw a very wild party at the Ritz Hotel. Mick was there with Bianca, and everyone got very drunk.

[flexibility]

Creamy garlic dip

This dip is a **perfect nibble** for when you have friends around, or just fancy an evening in front of the television.

Ⓥ *5 POINTS values per recipe* takes 15 minutes to prepare, 30 minutes to cook. Serves 6. Calories per serving 83. Freeze ✗

For the dip

1 whole bulb young garlic, unpeeled (see top tip)

½ teaspoon olive oil

150 g pot of 0% fat Greek yogurt

200 g (7 oz) low fat fromage frais

2 tablespoons chopped fresh chives

freshly ground black pepper

For the crudités

3 courgettes

low fat cooking spray

2 carrots, peeled and cut into batons

100 g (3½ oz) baby corn, halved lengthways

½ cucumber, cut into batons

1 red and 1 yellow pepper, de-seeded and sliced

● Preheat the oven to Gas Mark 4/180°C/ fan oven 160°C. Slice the top off the bulb of garlic and place in the middle of a square of foil. Drizzle the olive oil over the garlic and then wrap it in the foil. Place directly on to the oven shelf and bake for 30 minutes or until the garlic is soft.

● Remove the garlic from the oven and allow to cool slightly. Squeeze out the softened garlic from the papery skin into a bowl, then mash to a paste using a fork. Mix together with the yogurt and fromage frais, stir in the chives and season. Chill for 30 minutes until ready to serve.

● Cut the courgettes in half and then cut each section into quarters lengthways. Lightly coat with low fat cooking spray and cook under a preheated grill or in a non stick frying pan for 2 minutes each side until browned.

● Arrange on a platter with the remaining raw vegetables and serve with the creamy garlic dip.

Watercress soup

This creamy soup is a great choice to fill you up and keep you satisfied for very few *POINTS* values.

Ⓥ *5 POINTS values per recipe* takes 30 minutes to prepare. Serves 4. Calories per serving 126. Freeze ❄

2 teaspoons low fat polyunsaturated
  margarine, e.g. Flora Light
3 leeks, trimmed, rinsed and sliced
350 g (12 oz) potatoes, peeled and diced
1 litre (1¾ pints) vegetable stock, made using
  2 low salt stock cubes
75 g (2¾ oz) watercress
150 ml (¼ pint) skimmed milk
freshly ground black pepper

● Melt the margarine in a large saucepan. Stir in the leeks to coat, then add 2 tablespoons water, cover the pan and cook gently for 5 minutes.

● Add the potatoes and stock, bring the soup to the boil, cover and simmer for 15 minutes or until the potatoes are tender.

● Stir the watercress into the pan and add the milk, then liquidise the soup in batches and return to the pan. Gently reheat the soup and season with black pepper before serving.

5 a day

Watercress is rich in minerals such as iron and calcium plus beta-carotene and vitamin C. Adding the watercress to this soup just before blending preserves both its colour and its mineral content.

Top tip

Swirl 1 tablespoon of low fat fromage frais into each bowl of soup to make it extra creamy. This will add a POINTS value of ½ per serving.

2 POINTS VALUE

Mediterranean fish soup

Fish is a fabulous source of protein and contains lots of vitamins and minerals while being low in saturated fat.

If you're looking for a comforting meal, this hearty soup is packed with flavour, it's a complete meal in a bowl.

12 POINTS values per recipe takes 20 minutes to prepare, 30 minutes to cook. Serves 6. Calories per serving 166. Freeze ✗

1 red and 1 yellow pepper, quartered and de-seeded
1 tablespoon olive oil
1 large onion, sliced thinly
1/2 fennel bulb, sliced thinly
100 ml (3 1/2 fl oz) white wine
3 garlic cloves, sliced finely
juice and zest of 1 small orange
a pinch of saffron threads
850 ml (1 1/2 pints) fish stock, made using 1 low salt stock cube
230 g can of chopped tomatoes
200 g (7 oz) baby new potatoes, quartered
250 g (9 oz) boneless, skinless white fish fillet (e.g. monkfish or coley), chopped roughly
250 g (9 oz) frozen mixed seafood, defrosted
1 tablespoon chopped fresh parsley
freshly ground black pepper

Top tip

For a Mediterranean vegetable soup, use vegetable stock instead of fish stock, omit the fish fillet and mixed seafood, and add two diced courgettes along with the grilled peppers. This will reduce the POINTS value to 1 per serving.

● Preheat the grill and place the peppers on the grill rack, skin side up. Grill for 6–8 minutes until the skin is blistered. Transfer to a bowl, cover and cool for 10 minutes or so, then peel off the skin and roughly chop the peppers.

● While the peppers are grilling, heat the olive oil in a large saucepan. Stir in the onion and fennel and cook gently for 10 minutes until softened, but not coloured.

● Increase the heat, pour in the wine and stir in the garlic. Cook for about 2 minutes or until the wine has evaporated.

● Add the orange juice and zest, the saffron, fish stock, tomatoes and new potatoes. Season with black pepper to taste and bring to a simmer, cover and cook for 20 minutes.

● Stir the peppers and any juices that have collected in the bowl into the pan, along with the chopped fish. Replace the lid and gently poach for 3 minutes.

● Finally, stir in the mixed seafood and heat through for 2 minutes. Serve ladled into warmed bowls and scatter the parsley on top.

4 POINTS VALUE

Warm Puy lentil salad

This warm salad is full of contrasting textures and flavours. If you are cooking for one, the second portion makes a great lunchbox solution, served cold.

Ⓥ *8 POINTS values per recipe* takes 10 minutes to prepare, 20 minutes to cook. Serves 2. Calories per serving 274. Freeze ✗

80 g (3 oz) Puy lentils, rinsed
125 g (4¹/₂ oz) cooked natural beetroot, not
  in vinegar
low fat cooking spray
1¹/₂ tablespoons balsamic vinegar
¹/₂ teaspoon coarse-grain mustard
¹/₂ teaspoon walnut oil or extra virgin olive oil
65 g (2¹/₄ oz) mixed leaf salad
6 radishes, halved
50 g (1³/₄ oz) feta cheese, crumbled

● Preheat the oven to Gas Mark 6/200°C/ fan oven 180°C.

● Cook the lentils in boiling water for 15–20 minutes until tender but not mushy. Drain and rinse briefly with cold water.

● Meanwhile, drain the beetroot and cut into wedges. Place in a small roasting tin, coat with low fat cooking spray and drizzle with half a tablespoon of balsamic vinegar. Roast for 15 minutes or until caramelized around the edges.

● Whisk the remaining balsamic vinegar together with the mustard in a small bowl. Measure out 1 teaspoon of the mixture in a large bowl and whisk in the walnut or olive oil. Toss the salad leaves in the dressing until lightly coated and divide between two bowls or plates. Add the radishes.

● Mix the rest of the balsamic mixture with the drained lentils and spoon on to the plates. Scatter the roasted beetroot and feta over the salad and serve immediately.

Cooked lentils and pulses are a great source of protein for vegetarians. A single serving (3 heaped tablespoons) counts as 1 portion towards your 5 a day. However, even if you eat more than this they only count as 1 a day because, although they contain lots of healthy fibre, they don't provide as wide a variety of vitamins, minerals and other nutrients as fruit and vegetables.

Top tip

Nut and seed oils such as walnut oil are strongly flavoured, so a very small amount goes a long way in a salad dressing, yet delivers a big hit in terms of flavour.

2 POINTS VALUE Spicy prawn cakes

Great for a **dinner party starter or nibble**, these yummy prawn cakes can be made ahead and simply reheated just before your guests arrive.

7½ POINTS values per recipe takes 20 minutes + 30 minutes chilling. Serves 4. Calories per serving 136. Freeze ✗

For the prawn cakes

200 g (7 oz) frozen raw peeled tiger prawns, defrosted

200 g (7 oz) boneless skinless, white fish fillets (e.g. monkfish or coley), chopped roughly

1 tablespoon red Thai curry paste

1 tablespoon cornflour

4 spring onions, sliced finely

low fat cooking spray

For the dipping sauce

juice of 1 lime

4 tablespoons sweet chilli sauce

1 heaped tablespoon chopped fresh coriander

● Place the prawns, white fish, curry paste and cornflour in a food processor and blend until quite finely chopped. Remove the mixture from the food processor and place in a bowl. Mix in the spring onions and then cover and chill the mixture in the fridge for 30 minutes.

● To make the dipping sauce, mix the lime juice, chilli sauce and coriander together in a small bowl. Set aside.

● Using your hands, carefully shape the prawn mixture into 12 small cakes. Spray a large non stick frying pan with the low fat cooking spray and place on a medium to high heat. Add six prawn cakes and fry for 2 minutes on each side until browned and firm. Keep warm while you cook the remaining prawn cakes. Serve with the dipping sauce.

Top tip

To reheat, spread out in a single layer on a baking tray, cover with foil and heat through for 10 minutes in an oven preheated to Gas Mark 4/180°C/fan oven 160°C.

Mediterranean vegetable and pesto filling

A **versatile filling** for sandwiches and wraps, this also makes a lovely topping for a jacket potato.

(V) *3 POINTS values per recipe* takes 20 minutes. Serves 2. Calories per serving 125. Freeze ✗

2 small courgettes, trimmed and sliced thinly, lengthways

½ red and ½ yellow pepper, de-seeded and sliced lengthways

4 spring onions, trimmed and each cut into 2 short sections

low fat cooking spray

1 tablespoon pesto sauce

60 g (2 oz) plain low fat soft cheese

● Preheat the grill on a high setting. Lightly coat all the vegetables with low fat cooking spray, then cook the vegetables for about 4–5 minutes on each side, until tender and browned.

● While the vegetables are cooking, mix the pesto into the soft cheese. To serve, as photographed here, spread the pesto soft cheese on to a medium slice of wholemeal bread, then top with the chargrilled vegetables. This will be 2½ **POINTS** values per serving.

Fridge laundry

Chuck out the full fat soft cheese from your fridge and replace it with low fat or extra light versions which contain a fraction of the fat content, but with very little difference in flavour.

Top tip

Watch out for labels that say 'light' – some of these are medium fat soft cheese. Extra light versions are usually low fat soft cheese.

Low fat yogurt is often
an ideal alternative to
cream or soured cream

 Tzatziki chicken pittas

These Greek-style pittas are a **tasty alternative** to a kebab, which is traditionally high in **POINTS** values. The longer the chicken is marinated before cooking, the more the flavour will develop.

9 POINTS values per recipe takes 30 minutes + marinating. Serves 2. Calories per serving 426. Freeze ✗

50 g (1³/4 oz) low fat plain yogurt
75 g (2³/4 oz) 0% fat Greek yogurt
1 tablespoon chopped fresh mint
¹/2 teaspoon dried mint
1 small garlic clove, crushed
2 x 100 g (3¹/2 oz) boneless, skinless chicken
    breast fillets
4 cm (1¹/2-inch) piece of cucumber, diced
2 wholemeal pitta breads
1 large tomato, sliced

● Mix the two types of yogurt together with the fresh mint, dried mint and garlic. Set half of the mixture aside to make the tzatziki and pour the other half into a plastic food bag. Cut four shallow slashes in the top of each chicken breast using a sharp knife then place in the bag with the yogurt mixture. Squeeze out the excess air and seal. Place the bag in the fridge and marinate for at least 30 minutes.

● Mix the diced cucumber into the reserved yogurt mixture and chill the tzatziki until ready to serve.
● Preheat the grill on a medium setting. Remove the chicken from its marinade and cook under the grill for 7–8 minutes on each side. The juices should run clear when the thickest part of the breast is pierced.
● Place the chicken on a clean chopping board and let it rest for 5 minutes. Warm the pitta breads under a medium grill (or in the toaster) for 45–60 seconds on each side.
● Slice the chicken and transfer to a warmed serving plate. Split the pittas open, spoon in some tzatziki and fill with the chicken and tomato slices.

Top tip

Fresh and dried mint give very different flavours to this recipe, but if you don't have any fresh mint to hand you can simply increase the dried mint to 1 teaspoon.

6 POINTS VALUE

Creamy red pepper spaghetti

This creamy, cheesy sauce tastes really luxurious. The roasted peppers have a lovely sweet flavour, which is really brought to life in this dish.

Ⓥ *12 POINTS values per recipe* takes 20 minutes. Serves 2. Calories per serving 380. Freeze ✗

175 g (6 oz) wholemeal quick cook spaghetti
2 courgettes, trimmed and sliced into rounds
low fat cooking spray
2 roasted red peppers in brine, drained and
**   sliced**
60 g (2 oz) low fat garlic and herb soft cheese
15 g (½ oz) grated Parmesan cheese
freshly ground black pepper
2 tablespoons fresh basil leaves

● Cook the spaghetti in a large saucepan of boiling water for 10–12 minutes or until tender.

● Meanwhile, preheat the grill or a non stick frying pan. Lightly coat the courgettes with low fat cooking spray and then grill or fry for 2–3 minutes on each side until browned.

● Place three quarters of the sliced peppers in a blender with the soft cheese and 2 tablespoons of the pasta cooking water. Blend to a smooth sauce.

● Drain the pasta into a colander. Pour the pepper sauce into the pan, add the remaining sliced peppers and heat through gently. Mix the pasta and Parmesan into the sauce and season with freshly ground black pepper.

● Divide the spaghetti and sauce between two warmed bowls, then scatter the courgettes on top and garnish with basil leaves. Serve immediately.

> **Full factor**
>
> *Quick cook spaghetti has thinner strands than the regular type, so the same portion size in terms of **POINTS** values looks like a more generous serving. It also makes you feel more full, as it takes longer to eat.*

> **Top tip**
>
> *If you are feeling extra hungry, or simply want to add an extra portion of vegetables towards your 5 a day, add 150 g (5½ oz) small broccoli florets when cooking the spaghetti.*

Squash and red pepper risotto

4 POINTS VALUE

A perfect autumnal dish, this velvety risotto is really filling. Serve with lightly cooked green beans or sugar snap peas.

16½ POINTS values per recipe takes 40 minutes. Serves 4. Calories per serving 378. Freeze ✗

2 teaspoons olive oil

1 onion, chopped finely

1 large butternut squash, peeled, de-seeded and cut into 2 cm (³/4-inch) dice

2 red peppers, de-seeded and cut into 2 cm (³/4-inch) dice

1 garlic clove, crushed

low fat cooking spray

250 g (9 oz) risotto rice, e.g. Arborio

100 ml (3¹/2 fl oz) white wine

1 litre (1³/4 pints) vegetable stock, made using 2 low salt stock cubes

40 g (1¹/2 oz) plain low fat soft cheese

1 tablespoon chopped fresh thyme or lemon thyme

freshly ground black pepper

25 g (1 oz) wild rocket, to garnish

● Preheat the oven to Gas Mark 6/200°C/ fan oven 180°C. Heat the oil in a large saucepan and stir in the onion. Cover and cook gently for 8 minutes.

● While the onion softens, spread out the diced squash and peppers on a large roasting tray. Add the garlic, spray with low fat cooking spray and toss to coat. Roast in the oven for 20–25 minutes until caramelized around the edges, stirring once or twice during cooking.

● When the onion is ready, stir in the rice and cook for 1 minute. Pour in the wine and allow it to bubble until evaporated. Keeping the vegetable stock just simmering in another pan on the hob while you cook the risotto, add a ladleful of hot stock at a time to the rice, only adding the next one when the previous addition has been absorbed. Stir the rice every 2–3 minutes. It will take 20–25 minutes for the rice to cook through and absorb all of the stock.

● Stir the soft cheese into the risotto, followed by the thyme and roasted vegetables. Season with black pepper to taste and then divide between warmed bowls. Garnish with the wild rocket.

Smoked fish pie

4½ POINTS VALUE

A fantastic family favourite, this smoked fish pie is impressive enough to serve up when you are entertaining. Serve with a variety of zero vegetables.

27½ POINTS values per recipe takes 30 minutes to prepare, 25 minutes to cook. Serves 6. Calories per serving 355. Freeze ❄ (before cooking)

600 g (1 lb 5 oz) boneless smoked haddock fillet
500 ml (18 fl oz) skimmed milk
1.25 kg (2 lb 12 oz) floury potatoes (e.g. Desirée or Maris Piper), peeled and cut into chunks
2 tablespoons chopped fresh chives
1 tablespoon coarse-grain mustard (optional)
2 teaspoons low fat polyunsaturated margarine, e.g. Flora Light
3 leeks, trimmed, rinsed and sliced
100 g (3½ oz) smoked salmon, chopped roughly
2 tablespoons cornflour
½ low salt fish stock cube
juice of ½ a lemon
50 g (1¾ oz) plain low fat soft cheese
freshly ground black pepper

◦ Preheat the oven to Gas Mark 4/180°C/ fan oven 160°C. Place the smoked haddock in a roasting tin and season with pepper. Reserve 4 tablespoons of milk for the potato topping, then pour the remainder over the fish. Bake for 12 minutes or until the fish flakes easily. Carefully lift the fish,

using a fish slice, on to a plate to cool slightly and strain the milk into a jug.

◦ Meanwhile, cook the potatoes in a large saucepan of boiling water for 15–20 minutes or until tender. Drain and mash with the reserved 4 tablespoons of milk. Mix in the chives and the mustard, if using.

◦ While the potatoes are cooking, melt the margarine in a saucepan and stir in the leeks. Season with pepper and add 2 tablespoons of water. Cover and cook gently for 5 minutes.

◦ Using two forks, pull the smoked haddock away from its skin and break into large flakes. Place in a baking dish, add the smoked salmon and leeks and mix together.

◦ In a small bowl blend the cornflour with a little of the strained milk, then add back in to the rest of the milk and pour into the pan that the leeks were cooked in. Crumble in the fish stock cube and bring the sauce to a simmer, stirring until thickened. Simmer for 3 minutes, then whisk in the lemon juice and soft cheese until smooth. Pour this over the fish mixture and spread the mashed potatoes on top.

◦ Put the dish on a baking tray in the oven and cook for 25 minutes until golden.

Smoked fish is often quite salty naturally, so you shouldn't need to add any extra salt to this dish. Reducing the amount of salt that you eat can help to lower blood pressure and reduce the risk of strokes and heart attacks.

Top tip

Smoked salmon trimmings are a good option in this recipe, and will cost a lot less than the sliced version.

Spanish style garlic prawns

A super speedy recipe that's ideal for supper after work, or after a visit to the gym when you are hungry and want a **hot filling meal in a hurry**. Serve with 4 tablespoons of cooked brown rice for an extra 3 *POINTS* values.

2½ POINTS values per recipe takes 10 minutes. Serves 1. Calories per serving 252. Freeze ✗

a pinch of saffron threads

50 ml (2 fl oz) dry or medium sherry

1 teaspoon olive oil

1 yellow pepper, de-seeded and sliced

1 garlic clove, sliced

½ red chilli, de-seeded and sliced

230 g can of chopped tomatoes

100 g (3½ oz) frozen raw peeled tiger prawns
   (thoroughly defrosted)

1 tablespoon chopped fresh flat leaf parsley
   (optional)

freshly ground black pepper

- Crumble the saffron threads into the sherry and set aside until ready to use.
- Heat the oil in a non stick frying pan, add the pepper and fry for 2 minutes.
- Stir in the garlic and chilli and fry for 30 seconds or until the garlic is golden. Add the tomatoes, prawns and sherry mixture to the pan.
- Stir fry for 2–3 minutes or until the prawns are pink and firm. Scatter with the parsley before serving, if using. Season with freshly ground black pepper.

Top tip

Sherry gives this dish an authentically Spanish flavour, but if you don't like using alcohol, use vegetable stock instead. This will also save ½ POINTS value per serving.

(4 POINTS VALUE)

Tarragon chicken with lemon braised potatoes

An ideal recipe when you want a special meal for two that is really quick to prepare. Add some cooked broccoli florets to complete the meal.

8 POINTS values per recipe takes 10 minutes to prepare, 25 minutes to cook. Serves 2. Calories per serving 300. Freeze ✗

300 g (10½ oz) baby new potatoes, halved
300 ml (½ pint) chicken or vegetable stock, made using ½ low salt stock cube
juice and zest of ½ a lemon
2 tablespoons chopped fresh tarragon
3 tablespoons chopped fresh parsley
low fat cooking spray
2 x 150 g (5 oz) skinless, boneless chicken breast fillets
16 cherry tomatoes on the vine
¼ teaspoon granulated sugar
freshly ground black pepper

● Preheat the oven to Gas Mark 6/200°C/ fan oven 180°C. Place the potatoes in a saucepan with the stock, 1 tablespoon of lemon juice and ½ teaspoon of lemon zest. Bring to the boil and simmer, covered, for 15 minutes until tender.

● Meanwhile, mix the remaining lemon zest with the tarragon and 2 tablespoons parsley on a plate. Use a little low fat cooking spray on the chicken breasts and season them lightly. Roll the chicken in the herb mixture to coat completely and place in a lightly greased roasting tin. Drizzle the rest of the lemon juice over the chicken and cook in the oven for 10 minutes.

● Add the tomatoes to the roasting tin with the chicken, lightly coat with low fat cooking spray and sprinkle with the sugar. Return the roasting tin to the oven for 10 minutes, or until the chicken juices run clear when the thickest part of the breast is pierced with a sharp knife or skewer.

● When the potatoes are tender, remove the lid and increase the heat under the pan. Reduce the liquid for about 10 minutes or until it has almost all evaporated and you are left with about 2 tablespoons of syrupy juices. Toss the potatoes in the juices to glaze and scatter with the remaining parsley. Serve with the chicken and roasted tomatoes.

Tomatoes, especially when they are cooked, are a rich source of lycopene. This is an antioxidant and it may play an important part in the prevention of a variety of diseases, such as heart disease or certain cancers.

Top tip

Replace the chicken breasts with plain Quorn fillets for a vegetarian version. This will be 3½ **POINTS** values per serving.

Turkey patties with chilli apple sauce

You can make up these patties earlier in the day and leave them to chill in the fridge, ready for dinner time.

These **tasty** patties make a **delicious** lunch. Serve them with a crunchy zero salad.

17½ POINTS values per recipe takes 45 minutes + chilling. Serves 4. Calories per serving 263. Freeze ❄ (patties before cooking)

For the patties

75 g (2¾ oz) fresh wholemeal breadcrumbs (about 2 slices)

3 tablespoons skimmed milk

1 small onion, grated

1 teaspoon dried sage

1 small dessert apple, cored and diced finely

500 g (1 lb 2 oz) lean turkey mince

low fat cooking spray

1 tablespoon wholemeal plain flour

For the sauce

1 red chilli, de-seeded and diced

2 cooking apples, peeled, cored and chopped

1 tablespoon granulated sugar

● Combine the breadcrumbs and milk in a mixing bowl, then mix in the onion, sage, diced apple and turkey mince. Using your hands, carefully shape into 12 patties, cover and chill in the fridge for 30 minutes. Preheat the oven to Gas Mark 5/190°C/fan oven 170°C.

● Meanwhile make the sauce. Place the chilli, chopped cooking apples and 2 tablespoons of water in a saucepan. Cover and cook gently for 10 minutes, stirring occasionally, until the apples have softened to a purée. Remove from the heat and stir in the sugar.

● Lightly coat a non stick frying pan with low fat cooking spray. Dip the turkey patties in the flour to lightly coat them and brown for 1 minute on each side. Transfer to a baking tray lightly coated with low fat cooking spray and bake for 20 minutes. Serve with the chilli apple sauce.

Top tip

To make breadcrumbs let the bread dry out for 30 minutes on a wire rack, then tear into rough pieces and place in a food processor or mini blender to make crumbs. Adding softened breadcrumbs to the mixture gives a much better texture, and makes the meat go further.

Mushroom toad in the hole with onion gravy

A firm family favourite, with added vegetables to increase your daily intake.

Ⓥ **22 POINTS values per recipe** takes 20 minutes to prepare, 35 minutes to cook. Serves 4. Calories per serving 351. Freeze ✗

1 tablespoon olive oil

200 g (7 oz) open-cap mushrooms

1 onion, cut into wedges

8 Quorn vegetarian sausages

125 g (4¹/₂ oz) wholemeal plain flour

1 egg

300 ml (¹/₂ pint) skimmed milk

salt and freshly ground black pepper

For the onion gravy

low fat cooking spray

1 onion, sliced thinly

500 ml (18 fl oz) vegetable stock, made using 1 low salt stock cube

2 tablespoons wholemeal plain flour

1 teaspoon Marmite

● Preheat the oven to Gas Mark 7/220°C/ fan oven 200°C. Pour the olive oil into a non stick roasting tin measuring 19 cm (7¹/₂ inches) x 23 cm (9 inches) and toss the mushrooms, onion wedges and sausages in the oil to coat. Cook for 10 minutes until golden.

● Meanwhile, sift the flour into a mixing bowl with a pinch of salt, tipping in any bran from the sieve. Make a well in the centre and break in the egg. Gradually whisk in the milk to give a smooth batter. Season with salt and pepper. Pour the batter over the sausages and vegetables and return to the oven to cook for 20–25 minutes, until the batter is risen, crisp and golden.

● To make the gravy, spray a medium saucepan with low fat cooking spray and fry the sliced onion for 5 minutes until well browned. If necessary, add a little water to prevent the onion from sticking. Add 3 tablespoons of the stock, cover the pan and cook gently for 10 minutes until the onion is completely soft.

● Stir in the flour, followed by the rest of the stock and the Marmite. Bring to the boil and simmer, uncovered for 5 minutes. Season with black pepper to taste and serve with the toad In the hole.

Top tip

Replace the vegetarian sausages with low fat pork sausages if you wish. The **POINTS** values will remain the same.

Low fat cooking spray
is very useful when you
are trying to reduce
the amount of fat you
consume. Just a spray
or two will coat a pan
and give it a non stick
surface when frying
meat, fish or vegetables.

Hungarian goulash

A comforting, **richly flavoured casserole** that is wonderful served with a medium portion (150 g/5$\frac{1}{2}$ oz) of cooked tagliatelle and green cabbage, adding 2 **POINTS** values per serving.

15$\frac{1}{2}$ POINTS values per recipe takes 25 minutes to prepare, 2 hours to cook. Serves 4. Calories per serving 250. Freeze ❄ (without crème fraîche)

low fat cooking spray

450 g (1 lb) diced lean beef stewing steak

2 onions, sliced

2 garlic cloves, crushed

1 tablespoon paprika

1 tablespoon wholemeal plain flour

400 g can of chopped tomatoes

1 tablespoon tomato purée

**425 ml (15 fl oz) beef stock, made using 1 low
salt stock cube**

1 red and 1 green pepper, de-seeded and sliced

2 tablespoons half fat crème fraîche

freshly ground black pepper

● Preheat the oven to Gas Mark 1/140°C/ fan oven 120°C. Heat a flameproof casserole dish and spray with low fat cooking spray. Add the beef and fry until browned.

● At the same time, in a non stick frying pan, brown the onions using low fat cooking spray for 4–5 minutes, adding a little water if necessary to prevent the onions from sticking. Stir in the garlic, paprika and flour and cook for 30 seconds, then add the chopped tomatoes and tomato purée. Pour over the beef, add the stock and stir well to mix together.

● Bring to a simmer, then cover the casserole with a lid and cook in the oven for 1$\frac{1}{4}$ hours. Stir in the peppers, replace the lid and cook for a further 45 minutes. Remove from the oven, season with pepper and lightly stir in the crème fraîche to give a marbled effect.

Lemon and ginger sponge puddings

These steamed sponge puddings make the perfect finish to Sunday lunch and are served with a luscious lemon sauce.

(Y) **22 POINTS values per recipe** takes 20 minutes to prepare, 25 minutes to cook. Serves 4. Calories per serving 284. Freeze ❄ (puddings only)

low fat cooking spray
4 thin slices lemon
60 g (2 oz) low fat polyunsaturated margarine,
     e.g. Flora Light
60 g (2 oz) caster sugar
juice and zest of 1 lemon
1 egg, beaten
100 g (3¹/2 oz) wholemeal self raising flour,
     sifted
¹/2 teaspoon baking powder
¹/4 teaspoon ground ginger
2 tablespoons skimmed milk
2 pieces stem ginger in syrup, drained and diced
1 tablespoon cornflour
2 tablespoons of ginger syrup from the jar
1 tablespoon clear honey

● Lightly coat the inside of four mini pudding basins (150 ml/¹/4 pint) with low fat cooking spray. Place a lemon slice in the bottom of each basin. Cut 4 pieces of foil, each about 15 cm (6 inches) square and set aside with the prepared basins.

● Cream the margarine, sugar and lemon zest together in a mixing bowl, using an electric whisk, until pale and fluffy; then gradually beat in the egg. Sift the flour, baking powder and ground ginger over the mixture and fold in with a large metal spoon. Next fold in the milk, stem ginger and 1 tablespoon of the lemon juice.

● Divide the mixture between the pudding basins then cover each one with a square of foil, crimping it tightly under the lip of the basin. Place the puddings in a tiered steamer (see top tip), add boiling water to the base pan, cover tightly and steam for 25 minutes.

● Meanwhile, blend the cornflour with the remaining lemon juice in a saucepan then add 200 ml (7 fl oz) cold water, followed by the ginger syrup and honey. When the puddings have cooked for 20 minutes, gradually bring the sauce to the boil, stirring frequently, until the sauce has thickened and become clear.

● Unmould the sponge puddings with the aid of a small round knife and serve with the hot lemon sauce poured over.

Fridge laundry

Try switching to wholemeal flour for your baking; the extra fibre and other nutrients will do you good, and the results are just as light and fresh as with a more highly refined white flour.

Top tip

If you don't have a steamer, these puddings can be cooked in the oven, although the result won't be quite as light. Preheat the oven to Gas Mark 4/180°C/fan oven 160°C. Place the covered pudding basins on a baking tray and bake for 15 minutes until risen and firm to the touch.

Chocolate and pear layer cake

You can really enjoy this **light chocolate sponge with a creamy filling**, without having to worry about the fat content.

(Y) *15½ POINTS values per recipe* takes 20 minutes to prepare + cooling, 15 minutes to cook. Serves 6. Calories per serving 183. Freeze ❄ (sponge only, before adding filling)

For the cake

40 g (1½ oz) wholemeal plain flour

2 tablespoons cocoa powder

110 g (4 oz) caster sugar

5 large egg whites

a pinch of salt

¼ teaspoon cream of tartar

1 teaspoon vanilla extract

For the filling

250 g (9 oz) Quark

1 teaspoon vanilla extract

1 tablespoon granulated artificial sweetener

411 g can of pear slices in natural juice, drained

1 teaspoon icing sugar

● Preheat the oven to Gas Mark 4/180°C/fan oven 160°C. Line a 20 cm (8 inch) x 30 cm (12 inch) Swiss roll tin with baking parchment.

● Sift together the flour, cocoa powder and sugar, holding the sieve high to incorporate as much air as possible.

● In a large mixing bowl, whisk the egg whites until they are foamy, then add the salt and the cream of tartar. Continue beating until they form stiff peaks. Sift the flour mixture over the egg whites and add the vanilla extract. Use a large metal spoon to gently fold the ingredients together until smooth, making sure that there are no pockets of flour left in the mixture.

● Pour the batter into the prepared tin and level the surface using a palette knife. Bake for 15 minutes, or until the sponge feels firm and springy to the touch. Remove from the oven and turn out the cake on to a wire rack. Leave to cool.

● To make the filling, mix the Quark with the vanilla extract and sweetener. When the cake is cool, peel away the baking parchment and cut the cake into three equal rectangular sections, each 10 x 20 cm (4 x 8 inches). Place one section on a serving plate, spread with half the Quark mixture and add half the pears. Spread the remaining Quark on another piece of cake and stack on top, adding the rest of the pears. Top with the last section of cake and dust with icing sugar.

Apple strudel

British-grown Bramley apples are a **great seasonal ingredient**. When combined with spices and dried fruit they make a delicious strudel filling. Serve with a scoop of low fat vanilla ice cream for an additional *POINTS* value of 1.

Ⓥ *14 POINTS values per recipe* takes 20 minutes to prepare, 30 minutes to cook. Serves 6. Calories per serving 219. Freeze ❄

750 g (1 lb 10 oz) cooking apples, peeled, cored
    and diced
juice and zest of ½ a lemon
1 teaspoon ground cinnamon
60 g (2 oz) soft light brown sugar
50 g (1¾ oz) sultanas
25 g (1 oz) fresh wholemeal breadcrumbs
4 large sheets frozen filo pastry, defrosted
25 g (1 oz) low fat polyunsaturated margarine
    e.g. Flora Light, melted
1 teaspoon icing sugar

● Preheat the oven to Gas Mark 4/180°C/fan oven 160°C. In a mixing bowl, toss the diced apples with the lemon juice and zest, then mix in the cinnamon, sugar, sultanas and breadcrumbs. Set this aside.

● Lay a clean tea towel flat on the work surface and place two sheets of filo pastry on it side by side, like the pages of a book, making sure that they overlap by 2.5 cm (1 inch). Brush lightly with the melted margarine then layer the remaining filo on top as before, but placing the pastry at right angles to the first two sheets, overlapping slightly. Brush with a little more margarine.

● Heap the filling along the edge of the pastry nearest to you, leaving a gap of 5 cm (2 inches) at each end.

● Lightly grease a baking tray. Lifting the nearest edge of the tea towel up and away from you, roll the pastry tightly around the filling, tucking in the ends as you go so that the apple filling won't fall out. Lift up the strudel, still on the tea towel, then carefully tip it on to the baking tray, with the seam tucked underneath.

● Brush with any leftover melted margarine and bake for 30 minutes until the pastry is golden and the apples in the filling feel tender when pierced with a skewer. Dust with the icing sugar before serving.

Oaty peach crumble

This **comforting** crumble makes use of canned fruit so that you can prepare a **hot pudding** for the family, even when you are in a hurry.

19½ *POINTS values per recipe* takes 10 minutes to prepare, 25 minutes to cook Serves 4. Calories per serving 321. Freeze ✗

2 x 411 g cans of peach slices in natural juice
50 g (1¾ oz) low fat polyunsaturated margarine, e.g. Flora Light
100 g (3½ oz) wholemeal plain flour, sifted
25 g (1 oz) soft light brown sugar
2 tablespoons artificial granulated sweetener
1 teaspoon ground cinnamon
75 g (2¾ oz) porridge oats

● Preheat the oven to Gas Mark 4/180°C/fan oven 160°C. Drain the juice from the peaches into a jug or bowl and set aside. Tip the peach slices into a baking dish and add 6 tablespoons of the juice.

● In a mixing bowl, rub the margarine into the flour. Stir in the sugar, sweetener, cinnamon and porridge oats. Sprinkle in 2 tablespoons peach juice and stir until the mixture just begins to form small clumps.

● Scatter the crumble over the peaches and bake in the oven for 25 minutes until the topping is crisp and golden.

Chocolate, rum and raisin pudding

Utterly delectable, this decadent hot chocolate pudding is wonderful served with a scoop of low fat ice cream for an extra *POINTS* value of 1.

Ⓥ *9 POINTS values per recipe* takes 15 minutes to prepare + 1 hour soaking, 20–25 minutes to cook. Serves 2. Calories per serving 299. Freeze ✗

25 g (1 oz) raisins

30 ml (1 fl oz) dark rum

2 tablespoons cocoa powder

25 g (1 oz) soft light brown sugar

200 ml (7 fl oz) skimmed milk

1 egg

¹/₂ teaspoon vanilla extract

2 slices wholemeal or white bread, diced into
**   2 cm (³/₄ inch) cubes, keep crusts on**

● Start this recipe an hour ahead by soaking the raisins in the rum until plump. When you are ready to make the pudding, preheat the oven to Gas Mark 4/180°C/fan oven 160°C.

● Place the cocoa powder and sugar in a saucepan and gradually blend in the milk, then bring the mixture up to simmering point. Remove from the heat.

● Whisk the egg and vanilla extract together in a bowl, then gradually pour in the warm chocolate milk, stirring all the time. Drain the raisins and add any rum

that hasn't been absorbed by the raisins.

● Place half the bread and drained raisins in a baking dish and pour over half the chocolate custard, straining it through a sieve to remove any eggy threads. Repeat with the remaining ingredients and push the bread down into the chocolate mixture. Let it stand for 5 minutes for the bread to absorb the chocolate custard, and put the kettle on to boil.

● Place the dish inside a roasting tin and pour enough boiling water around the dish to come about halfway up the sides. Bake in the oven on the centre shelf for 20–25 minutes – the pudding should be slightly risen and puffy, with a crisp top. Remove from the oven and allow it to stand for 5 minutes before serving.

Switching to skimmed milk from full fat milk will not only lower your fat intake, it will also increase the calcium in your diet, which helps to maintain strong bones and teeth and to guard against osteoporosis.

Top tip

Baking delicate egg custard recipes in a hot water bath helps to keep an even, gentle temperature that will ensure a velvety smooth texture. If the temperature gets too high, eggs are likely to become overcooked and rubbery.

NoCount

NoCount offers you the freedom to know exactly what you can eat, helping you to stay in control of your eating. The **NoCount** list contains foods that are low in energy density, offering a balanced, nutritious and healthy food plan. The following recipes offer interesting and delicious ways to make the most of the **NoCount** foods and will help you to lose weight, feel good and look great.

Japanese shiitake noodles (page 83)

[freedom]

Curried chicken pasta salad lunchbox

Wholemeal pasta is made
from wheat which hasn't
had all the outer bran
removed before it is
processed so it contains
a lot more fibre; this
plays an important
element in any healthy
eating plan. Don't be
put off by its 'worthy'
image though; it actually
has a light texture and a
lovely nutty flavour.

Substantial salads are ideal for NoCount lunches, whether you eat at home or at work. This **mildly spiced pasta salad** will keep you going all afternoon.

6½ *POINTS values per recipe* takes 20 minutes. Serves 1. Calories per serving 449. Freeze ✗

60 g (2 oz) dried pasta twists
low fat cooking spray
100 g (3½ oz) skinless, boneless chicken breast
½ teaspoon curry powder
a pinch of ground turmeric
1 teaspoon lemon juice
30 g (1¼ oz) plain low fat soft cheese
125 g (4½ oz) low fat plain yogurt
1 teaspoon granulated artificial sweetener
½ red, yellow or orange pepper, de-seeded and diced
2 spring onions, chopped roughly
2 tablespoons chopped fresh coriander

● Cook the pasta for 10–12 minutes in boiling water. Drain and rinse in cold water.

● Meanwhile, spray a non stick frying pan with low fat cooking spray and cook the chicken breast for 5 minutes on each side or until cooked through. Remove from the pan and slice when cooled.

● Mix the curry powder, turmeric and lemon juice together to make a paste. Blend in the low fat soft cheese until smooth. Add the yogurt and sweetener and mix together well.

● Stir in the remaining ingredients, including the pasta and chicken, until everything is well coated in the dressing. Transfer to a lunchbox, seal and chill until ready to serve.

Top tip

*For a vegetarian version, use 100 g (3½ oz) Quorn fillets in place of the chicken. This will still be a NoCount lunch and the **POINTS** values will then be 6 per serving.*

Spiced tomato and lentil soup

Stress free

Freeze in portions in advance so that you have a quick and easy, filling meal to hand in just a few minutes.

With plenty of fibre and protein from the lentils, this filling soup is a **great standby** to keep in the fridge for when you are short of time.

(Y) *7 POINTS values per recipe* takes 10 minutes to prepare, 30 minutes to cook. Serves 6. Calories per serving 123. Freeze ❄

1 onion, chopped finely

2 carrots, peeled and diced

150 g (5½ oz) red lentils, rinsed

2 x 400 g cans of chopped tomatoes

1 tablespoon ground cumin

1 teaspoon medium curry powder

1.2 litres (2 pints) vegetable stock, made using
**   2 low salt stock cubes**

3 tablespoons fresh chopped coriander

freshly ground black pepper

● Place all the ingredients except for the coriander in a large saucepan. Bring to a simmer, cover and cook for 30 minutes or until the lentils are completely soft.

● Let the soup cool slightly, then liquidise in batches in a blender. Season with black pepper to taste and serve with the coriander scattered on top.

Top tip

*This soup tastes fantastic with a spoonful of low fat plain yogurt, but remember that if you're following Full Choice you'll need to add a **POINTS** value of ½ per serving.*

Moroccan chicken soup

A cross between a soup and a stew, this **Moroccan delight** will satisfy all of your senses. If you want the soup to taste **really authentic**, add a dash of fiery Tabasco sauce before serving.

14¹/₂ POINTS values per recipe takes 45 minutes. Serves 4. Calories per serving 225. Freeze ❄ (before the final step)

low fat cooking spray
1 onion, chopped finely
2 garlic cloves, crushed
1 green chilli, de-seeded and diced
225 g (8 oz) chicken mince
1 teaspoon ground cinnamon
1 teaspoon ground cumin
¹/₂ teaspoon ground coriander
1.2 litres (2 pints) chicken stock, made using
   2 low salt stock cubes
410 g can of chickpeas, drained and rinsed
3 tablespoons tomato purée
50 g (1³/₄ oz) dry couscous
3 tablespoons fresh chopped mint
juice of 1 large lemon

- Heat a large saucepan and coat with low fat cooking spray. Add the onion and brown for 5 minutes, adding a little water if needed to stop the onions from sticking. Add the garlic, chilli and chicken mince and cook, stirring to break up the mince, until lightly coloured.
- Mix in the ground spices and cook for 30 seconds before adding the chicken stock, chickpeas and tomato purée. Bring to the boil, cover and simmer for 20 minutes.
- Remove from the heat and stir in the couscous, mint and lemon juice. Cover the pan and leave to stand for 5 minutes until the couscous is tender. Ladle into warmed bowls to serve.

Top tip

*For a vegetarian version of this soup, replace the chicken mince with minced Quorn and use vegetable stock instead of chicken stock. This will still be a NoCount meal and the **POINTS** values will remain the same.*

Smoked trout and potato salad

The combination of smoked trout and potatoes in a creamy mustard dressing tastes simply divine. This salad can be served slightly warm or, once it is cool, packed into a lunchbox to take to work the next day.

8¹/2 POINTS values per recipe takes 25 minutes. Serves 2. Calories per serving 281. Freeze ✗

350 g (12 oz) baby new potatoes, halved
100 g (3¹/2 oz) low fat plain fromage frais
2 teaspoons coarse-grain mustard
1 teaspoon Dijon mustard
6 cornichons (mini gherkins), diced finely
2 spring onions, sliced thinly
75 g (2³/4 oz) baby spinach leaves
125 g (4¹/2 oz) smoked trout fillets

- Cook the potatoes in boiling water for 15 minutes or until tender.
- Meanwhile, mix the fromage frais together with the two mustards, cornichons and spring onions to make the dressing.
- When the potatoes are ready, drain and leave them to cool for 5 minutes before mixing them with the dressing.
- Divide the spinach leaves between two bowls and spoon the potatoes on top. Break up the trout fillets into chunky flakes and scatter over the potatoes.

Super foods

Oily fish such as trout, salmon, mackerel and fresh tuna contain high levels of omega-3 fatty acids, which are types of polyunsaturated fatty acids that help to reduce the risk of heart disease.

Top tip

Cornichons are miniature pickled gherkins. They have a lovely sweet-sharp taste and add a crunchy texture to this salad.

Thai beef salad

Traditionally a Thai starter, this main meal sized salad is a wonderful combination of sweet and sharp flavours.

4 POINTS values per recipe takes 15 minutes. Serves 1. Calories per serving 284. Freeze ✗

125 g (4½ oz) piece of beef medallion or lean fillet steak at room temperature
low fat cooking spray
1 tablespoon Thai fish sauce or soy sauce
juice of ½ a lime
1 teaspoon grated fresh root ginger
4 cm (1½-inch) piece of cucumber, cut into matchsticks
50 g (1¾ oz) fresh beansprouts, rinsed
60 g (2 oz) seedless red grapes, halved
½ red chilli, de-seeded and sliced
1 tablespoon fresh mint leaves
30 g (1¼ oz) herb salad

- Preheat a chargrill pan or non stick frying pan on a high setting. Lightly spray the steak with low fat cooking spray and add to the pan. Cook it for 2 minutes on each side for rare or 3 minutes each side for medium rare. Remove the cooked steak to a plate and rest for 5 minutes before slicing thinly.

- Meanwhile, mix the fish or soy sauce with the lime juice in a salad bowl. Squeeze the grated ginger over the bowl to extract the juice and then discard the pulp. Toss the cucumber and beansprouts into the dressing. Add the grapes, chilli, mint leaves and herb salad and mix thoroughly.

- Arrange the steak on top of the salad, pouring any juices from the plate over the top. Serve immediately.

Top tip

For the best results, the steak should be cooked rare to medium rare in this recipe in order to keep the meat succulent and juicy.

Roasted vegetable couscous lunchbox

Super foods

Roasting vegetables in the oven really concentrates the flavour and brings out their **natural sweetness**. Mixed with couscous, they make for a **filling and flavoursome** lunch solution.

ⓨ *5 POINTS values per recipe* takes 35 minutes. Serves 2. Calories per serving 236. Freeze ✗

1 courgette, trimmed and cut into chunks
1 red and 1 yellow pepper, de-seeded and chopped roughly
1 small red onion, peeled and cut into 6 wedges
200 g (7 oz) butternut squash, peeled, deseeded and diced
low fat cooking spray
175 g (6 oz) cherry tomatoes
175 ml (6 fl oz) vegetable stock, made using ½ low salt stock cube, hot
100 g (3½ oz) dry couscous
1 tablespoon fresh chopped basil
25 g (1 oz) wild rocket

● Preheat the oven to Gas Mark 6/200°C/ fan oven 180°C. Toss the courgette, peppers, red onion and squash together in a large roasting tray, lightly coat the vegetables in low fat cooking spray and roast in the oven for 15 minutes, stirring half way through.
● Spray the cherry tomatoes with low fat cooking spray and add them to the tray of vegetables. Roast for a further 5 minutes, or until the vegetables are tender and beginning to caramelize around the edges.
● Meanwhile, pour the hot stock over the couscous in a bowl, stir once and then cover and leave to stand for 5 minutes until the couscous has absorbed the liquid. Fluff up the couscous and stir in the basil. Divide the couscous between two lunchboxes, top with the roasted vegetables and leave to cool.
● Add the wild rocket once the couscous and vegetables are cool. Seal and chill until ready to eat.

Peppers contain antioxidants such as vitamin C and also beta carotene, which may help to protect against heart disease, strokes and some cancers.

Top tip

Butternut squash can be tricky to peel, but a swivel headed vegetable peeler will make the job much easier.

Quick chilli bean jacket filling

If you want to double up the recipe and save one portion for another day, the chilli beans are also delicious served with rice or with home-made jacket wedges (see Top tip below).

Ⓨ *4 POINTS values per recipe* takes 10 minutes. Serves 1. Calories per serving 209. Freeze ❄

½ **small yellow or green pepper, de-seeded**
    and diced finely
low fat cooking spray
1 small garlic clove, crushed
a pinch of chilli powder
½ teaspoon ground cumin
230 g can of chopped tomatoes
½ x 410 g can of butter beans, drained
    and rinsed
2 tablespoons low fat plain fromage frais
1 tablespoon chopped fresh coriander

● Stir fry the diced pepper in low fat cooking spray for 3 minutes until browned. Add the garlic, chilli powder and cumin and cook for 30 seconds before mixing in the tomatoes and butter beans. Simmer for 5 minutes.

● Spoon onto a split jacket potato and top with the fromage frais and fresh coriander. Serve immediately.

Top tip

To make jacket wedges cut a baking potato into 8–10 wedges then parboil in vegetable stock for 6 minutes. Drain well then coat with low fat cooking spray and spread out on a roasting tray. Cook in a preheated oven at Gas Mark 6/ 200°C/fan oven 180°C for 25 minutes until crispy and golden, turning half way through.

One pot veggie curry

This delicious curry is crammed full of multi coloured vegetables to give a variety of nutrients. Any leftover curry is wonderful spooned over a crisp-skinned jacket potato the next day.

A serving of vegetables is 80 g (3 oz) in weight. This is equivalent to about 8 cauliflower florets, half a pepper or 4 heaped tablespoons of green beans. Fresh, frozen and canned vegetables all count as part of your 5 a day. However, potatoes don't count towards this target as they are considered a 'starchy' food like rice, pasta and bread.

10½ POINTS values per recipe takes 15 minutes to prepare, 20 minutes to cook Serves 4. Calories per serving 253. Freeze ✗

1 onion, chopped roughly
low fat cooking spray
1 red and 1 yellow pepper, de-seeded and
    chopped roughly
2 teaspoons grated root ginger
2 garlic cloves, crushed
1 tablespoon medium curry powder
500 g (1 lb 2 oz) potatoes, peeled and diced
225 g (8 oz) cauliflower florets
850 ml (1½ pints) vegetable stock using 2 low
    salt stock cubes
110 g (4 oz) red lentils, rinsed
150 g (5½ oz) green beans, trimmed and cut
    into thirds
freshly ground black pepper
chopped fresh coriander, to serve

Brown the onion using low fat cooking spray in a large saucepan or flameproof casserole dish, for 2 minutes. Tip the peppers into the pan and stir fry for a further 2 minutes. Stir in the ginger, garlic and curry powder and cook for 30 seconds.

Add the potatoes and cauliflower to the pan and stir to coat in the spice mixture, then pour in the vegetable stock and lentils. Mix together well and season lightly. Bring the mixture to a simmer, cover the pan and cook for 10 minutes.

Stir the green beans into the curry, replace the lid and cook gently for a further 10 minutes or until the lentils have broken down to thicken the sauce and the vegetables are tender. Scatter with coriander before serving.

9 POINTS VALUE

Roast monkfish wrapped in bacon

Pre-packed lean back
bacon can be quite
expensive, so buy
ordinary back bacon
rashers and trim away
all the fat with kitchen
scissors.

Perfect for a romantic meal for two, followed by Speedy Sticky Pears (see p 88).
Serve the monkfish and crispy potatoes with broccoli or fine green beans.

18 POINTS values per recipe takes 20
minutes to prepare, 30 minutes to cook
Serves 2. Calories per serving 494. Freeze ✗

low fat cooking spray
600 g (1 lb 5 oz) potatoes, peeled and cut into
5 mm (¼-inch) slices
juice and zest of ½ a lemon
2 x 225 g (8 oz) pieces monkfish tail, boned and
membrane removed
1 tablespoon fresh chopped parsley
8 fresh sage leaves
4 rashers lean back bacon
1 onion, sliced
freshly ground black pepper

○ Preheat the oven to Gas Mark 6/200°C/
fan oven 180°C and coat a large roasting
tray with low fat cooking spray.

○ Parboil the potatoes in boiling water for
4–5 minutes, until just tender. Drain and
spread them out on the roasting tray. Spray
with low fat cooking spray and cook in the
oven for 15 minutes.

○ Cut a pocket in each piece of monkfish
and stuff with the lemon zest and parsley.
Drizzle the lemon juice over the fish,
season and then wrap each piece tightly in
two rashes of bacon with the sage leaves
tucked inside.

○ When the potatoes have cooked for
15 minutes, add the onion and turn the
potato slices over using a fish slice. Sit the
monkfish wraps in amongst the potatoes
and spray with low fat cooking spray.
Return the tray to the oven to cook for a
further 15 minutes, or until the monkfish
feels firm to the touch.

Top tip

*This recipe can also be
prepared with other firm
white fish fillets such as
cod loin. The **POINTS**
value per serving will
remain the same.*

One tray roast chicken

An **easy mid week roast** that will please the whole family and get them eating their vegetables. With everything roasted together in one tray, it also saves on washing up!

21½ POINTS values per recipe takes 20 minutes to prepare, 30 minutes to cook. Serves 4. Calories per serving 403. Freeze ✗

600 g (1 lb 5 oz) baby new potatoes, halved
juice and zest of 1 lemon
2 tablespoons chopped fresh thyme or rosemary
2 garlic cloves, crushed
4 chicken breast quarters, skin removed (see Top tip)
4 leeks, trimmed, rinsed and each cut into 3 chunks
1 red and 1 yellow pepper, deseeded and chopped roughly
low fat cooking spray
200 g (7 oz) cherry tomatoes
freshly ground black pepper

- Preheat the oven to Gas Mark 6/200°C/ fan oven 180°C. Boil the potatoes in boiling water for 10 minutes, until just tender.
- Meanwhile, mix the lemon zest with the herbs and crushed garlic. Lightly slash the chicken quarters using a sharp knife and rub the herb mixture all over and into the chicken.
- Drain the potatoes well and tip them into a large roasting tin. Add the leeks and peppers and spray the vegetables with low fat cooking spray. Arrange the chicken joints on top, drizzle the lemon juice over and season lightly with black pepper.
- Roast for 10 minutes, stir everything around, then return the tin to the oven for a further 10 minutes. Add the cherry tomatoes and stir again so that everything browns evenly, and then roast for a final 10 minutes. Check that the chicken is cooked through by piercing the thickest part of the joints with a sharp knife: the juices should run clear.

Top tip

It's much easier to skin chicken joints If you grasp the skin with kitchen paper. This gives you a better grip, enabling you to easily pull the skin away from the flesh.

Cajun pork steaks with sweet potato chips

If you're looking for something different to serve next time you have friends around for dinner, this recipe will prove a talking point. The tropical flavours of the salsa perfectly complement the spicy pork steaks and caramelised sweet potato chips.

31½ POINTS values per recipe takes 25 minutes to prepare, 30 minutes to cook Serves 4. Calories per serving 524. Freeze ✗

low fat cooking spray
1.25 kg (2 lb 12 oz) sweet potatoes, peeled and
 cut into wedges
½ low salt vegetable stock cube
4 x 175 g (6 oz) pork loin steaks
juice of 1 lime and zest of ½ lime
2 teaspoons Cajun spice powder
½ pineapple, peeled, cored and chopped finely
½ red pepper, de-seeded and diced
½ green chilli, de-seeded and diced

● Preheat the oven to Gas Mark 6/ 200°C/ fan oven 180°C. With a kitchen towel lightly coat a baking tray with low fat cooking spray.

● Cook the sweet potato wedges in boiling water with the vegetable stock cube, for 5 minutes. Drain the potatoes, spread out on the baking tray and spray with low fat cooking spray. Cook in the oven for 25–30 minutes, turning half way through.

● Trim the fat from the pork steaks then pat them dry on kitchen towel. Place on a plate, drizzle half the lime juice over them and sprinkle the Cajun spice on both sides of each steak. Set aside and preheat the grill on a medium to high setting.

● Mix the remaining lime juice and zest together with the pineapple, red pepper and chilli in a small serving bowl.

● Grill the pork steaks for 12–15 minutes, or until they are cooked through and the juices run clear. Serve with the sweet potato chips and the pineapple salsa spooned over the pork.

To prepare a pineapple, firstly slice off the base and the leaves of the pineapple. Stand the pineapple upright and cut into wedges. Trim away the core from each wedge, and then slice the flesh away from the skin, as if you were preparing a melon.

Rosemary lamb casserole

Rosemary and lamb are a classic combination and this slow cooked casserole gives a melt-in-the-mouth result. The beans absorb all the delicious flavours of the sauce as it cooks.

26½ POINTS values per recipe takes 15 minutes to prepare, 1½ hours to cook
Serves 4. Calories per serving 244.
Freeze ❄

450 g (1 lb) lean diced casserole lamb
low fat cooking spray
1 onion, sliced
2 garlic cloves, crushed
1 tablespoon fresh chopped rosemary or 1
    teaspoon dried rosemary
425 ml (15 fl oz) lamb or vegetable stock,
    made using 1 low salt stock cube
1 tablespoon tomato purée
410 g can of cannellini, butter or haricot beans,
    drained and rinsed
200 g (7 oz) cherry tomatoes
freshly ground black pepper

● Preheat the oven to Gas Mark 1/140°C/ fan oven 120°C. Heat a flameproof casserole dish on the hob and brown the lamb in low fat cooking spray in batches, removing the meat to a plate as it is browned.

● Add the onion to the casserole dish and brown for 4 minutes, adding a splash of water if needed to stop the onion sticking. Stir in the garlic and rosemary and cook for 30 seconds before adding the stock, tomato purée and a generous seasoning of pepper.

● Return the lamb to the casserole dish. Bring it all to a simmer, cover and transfer to the oven to cook for 1 hour.

● Stir the beans of your choice, together with the cherry tomatoes, into the casserole, replace the lid and cook for a further 30 minutes.

Top tip

If it's more convenient to use dried herbs rather than fresh, remember that the flavour is more concentrated so you will only need 1 teaspoon of dried herbs to replace 1 tablespoon of fresh.

One pot Italian beef stew

*Once the preparation
is out of the way, just
pop the stew in the
oven while you
prepare other things.*

This is a great all-in-one filling family casserole, containing meat, vegetables and pasta.

22¹/₂ POINTS values per recipe takes 25 minutes to prepare, 1³/₄ hours to cook. Serves 4. Calories per serving 315. Freeze ❄ (before adding the pasta)

600 g (1 lb 5 oz) diced lean beef stewing steak
low fat cooking spray
1 large onion, sliced
6 garlic cloves, peeled
1 tablespoon fresh chopped rosemary
12 black olives in brine, drained
400 g can of chopped tomatoes
1 litre (1³/₄ pints) beef stock made using 2 low
    salt stock cubes
125 g (4¹/₂ oz) wholemeal pasta shapes, e.g.
    fusilli
freshly ground black pepper

▪ Preheat the oven to Gas Mark 1/140°C/ fan oven 120°C. Brown the beef in low fat cooking spray in a non stick frying pan. Do this in two batches, transferring the meat to a plate as it is done.

▪ At the same time, brown the onion in low fat cooking spray in a large flameproof casserole dish, adding a splash of water if needed to stop the onion from sticking.

▪ Add the whole garlic cloves, rosemary, olives and chopped tomatoes to the casserole dish. Pour a little of the stock into the frying pan and stir to release the meat browning juices, then add this to the casserole, along with the rest of the stock. Return the beef to the casserole and bring it to a simmer. Cover and transfer to the oven to cook for 1¹/₂ hours.

▪ Stir the pasta into the casserole, pushing it down into the liquid. Replace the lid and return the casserole to the oven to cook for 15–20 minutes, until the pasta is tender. Season and serve immediately.

Japanese shiitake noodles

This Japanese style noodle stir fry can be on the table in 15 minutes or less when you're in need of a **speedy but wholesome** home-cooked meal.

3 POINTS values per recipe takes 15 minutes. Serves 1. Calories per serving 203. Freeze ✗

low fat cooking spray
150 g (5½ oz) shiitake mushrooms, halved
   through the stalk
1 small garlic clove, sliced finely
1 teaspoon shredded fresh root ginger
6 spring onions, trimmed and cut into thirds
2 tablespoons soy sauce, preferably Japanese
100 g (3½ oz) pak choi, separated into leaves
60 g (2 oz) soba noodles or medium egg
   noodles

● Coat a medium saucepan with low fat cooking spray then add the mushrooms, garlic, ginger and spring onions and stir fry for 3 minutes until browned.

● Add the soy sauce and 100 ml (3½ fl oz) water to the pan, bring to the boil and cook, stirring, for 5 minutes, uncovered, until around 3 tablespoons of syrupy liquid remain. Add the pak choi to the pan, cover and cook for 2 minutes or until the leaves begin to wilt.

● Meanwhile, cook the noodles as per packet instructions. Drain the noodles and then toss together with the vegetables. Serve immediately.

Top tip

*If shiitake mushrooms and pak choi aren't available, substitute chestnut mushrooms and roughly chopped Chinese leaf for a perfectly good alternative. This will still be a NoCount meal and the **POINTS** values will stay the same if following Full Choice.*

7 POINTS VALUE® **Teriyaki chicken skewers**

Skinless chicken thigh
fillets are slightly
higher in fat than
white breast meat,
but they are less prone
to drying out during
cooking and stay
juicy and succulent,
especially if the meat is
marinated beforehand.

Ready made teriyaki marinade gives the chicken **plenty of flavour** and is available in most supermarkets. It has a consistency similar to soy sauce. Serve with 2 tablespoons of rice for a *POINTS* value of 1¹/₂, if following Full Choice.

14¹/₂ POINTS values per recipe takes 30 minutes + marinating. Serves 2. Calories per serving 240. Freeze ✗

6 tablespoons teriyaki marinade
4 skinless, boneless chicken thigh fillets
10 chestnut or shiitake mushrooms, halved
    through the stalk
6 spring onions, trimmed and cut into 4 cm
    (1¹/₂-inch) lengths

● Measure the teriyaki marinade into a large plastic food bag, place inside a bowl to avoid spillage.
● Cut each chicken thigh fillet into four or five chunky pieces and put them in the marinade in the bag, along with the mushrooms and spring onions. Squeeze the excess air out of the bag and seal tightly. All of the ingredients should now be in close contact with the marinade. Marinate in the fridge for at least 1 hour.
● Soak four wooden skewers in cold water for at least 10 minutes to prevent them from burning during cooking.
● Preheat the grill to high, and line the grill pan with foil. Thread the chicken and vegetables on the skewers. Grill for 12–15 minutes, turning occasionally and brushing with the marinade.

Top tip

For a vegetarian alternative, replace the chicken with 300 g (10¹/2 oz) diced firm tofu or Quorn chunks. These will only take around 8 minutes to cook under the grill. This will still be NoCount and the **POINTS** *values will be 2 per serving.*

2½ POINTS VALUE

Lemon and berry creamy pots

If you're looking for a **sweet indulgence**, try this NoCount version of cheesecake – it's so luscious that you won't even miss the usual biscuit base.

9 POINTS values per recipe takes 15 minutes + chilling. Serves 4. Calories per serving 131. Freeze ✗

juice and zest of 1 lemon
12 g sachet of gelatine powder
200 g (7 oz) plain low fat soft cheese
250 g (9 oz) low fat plain yogurt
5 tablespoons granulated artificial sweetener
250 g (9 oz) frozen summer berries mix,
     defrosted

● Pour the lemon juice into a small heatproof bowl and sprinkle the gelatine over. Leave to stand for 3 minutes to absorb the liquid and then stand the bowl in a small saucepan of gently simmering water and leave to melt.

● Meanwhile, mix together the lemon zest, soft cheese, yogurt and 4 tablespoons of sweetener in a mixing bowl until smooth. Pour in the melted gelatine and stir to combine evenly.

● Divide the mixture between 4 x 200 ml (7 fl oz) glasses, cover with clingfilm and chill in the fridge for 1 hour or until firm.

● Mix the defrosted berries with the remaining sweetener and spoon on top of the pots just before serving.

Fridge laundry

This cheesecake is a great alternative to the traditional dessert, as it uses low fat soft cheese and comes without the usual high fat biscuit base.

Top tip

*For a strawberry version, replace the low fat plain yogurt with low fat strawberry yogurt, and top with 150 g (5½ oz) sliced strawberries. This will still be a NoCount dish and the **POINTS** values per serving will remain the same.*

Speedy sticky pears

A fantastically fast pudding fix, complete with a creamy accompaniment.

Ⓥ *3¹/₂ POINTS values per recipe* takes 5 minutes. Serves 2. Calories per serving 89. Freeze ✗

410 g can of pear halves in natural juice, drained

1¹/₂ teaspoons granulated artificial sweetener

low fat cooking spray

For the cinnamon fromage frais

100 g (3¹/₂ oz) low fat plain fromage frais

pinch of ground cinnamon

● Heat a non stick frying pan on a medium to high heat. Drain the pears on kitchen towel and sprinkle over half a teaspoon of the sweetener. Lightly coat the frying pan with low fat cooking spray, add the pears and cook for 2 minutes each side until caramelized.

● Meanwhile, mix the fromage frais together with the cinnamon and the remaining sweetener. Spoon over the caramelised pears to serve.

Baked nutmeg custard pots

These **velvety smooth** custard pots will increase your calcium intake, and can be served topped with drained canned apricots in natural juice (as in the photograph opposite). Sliced banana is a great accompaniment as are defrosted summer fruits.

8½ *POINTS values per recipe* takes 35 minutes. Serves 6. Calories per serving 100. Freeze ✗

425 ml (15 fl oz) skimmed milk
60 g (2 oz) plain low fat soft cheese
3 eggs + 1 egg yolk, beaten
1 teaspoon vanilla extract
5 tablespoons granulated artificial sweetener
¼ whole nutmeg

● Preheat the oven to Gas Mark 3/160°C/ fan oven 140°C. Gradually bring the milk up to simmering point in a saucepan, and put the kettle on to boil.

● Meanwhile, place the low fat soft cheese in a mixing bowl and slowly mix in the beaten eggs until smooth using a wooden spoon, so that the mixture doesn't become frothy, causing air bubbles in the custard pots.

● Slowly pour the hot milk over the egg mixture, mixing until smooth. Stir in the vanilla and sweetener.

● Place six ramekin dishes in a roasting tin and divide the egg mixture between them, pouring it through a sieve to remove any eggy threads that would spoil the texture. Grate plenty of fresh nutmeg on to the custards and then place the roasting tin in the oven. Pour boiling water into the tin around the ramekins and bake for about 20 minutes, until the custards feel just firm to the touch, but are still slightly wobbly in the centre.

● Carefully lift the ramekins out of the hot water bath using a fish slice. Let them cool slightly before eating them warm, or cool completely and then chill until ready to serve.

Top tip

If you don't have any ramekins, you can use heatproof tea cups or coffee cups to bake the individual custards in. Alternatively, you can bake all of the mixture in a single large shallow dish, which will take about 40 minutes to cook.

Apple snow

A light and fluffy fruity dessert that's easy to prepare ahead – and the perfect recipe for using up those windfall apples.

 4 POINTS values per recipe takes 20 minutes + chilling. Serves 4. Calories per serving 98. Freeze ✗

700 g (1 lb 9 oz) cooking apples, cored, peeled and chopped
1/2 teaspoon ground cinnamon
4 tablespoons granulated sweetener
100 g (3 1/2 fl oz) low fat plain yogurt
1 egg white
1 dessert apple, cored and sliced

● Place the cooking apples in a saucepan with the cinnamon and 2 tablespoons of water. Cover the pan and cook gently for 10 minutes, stirring occasionally, until the apples have softened to a purée. Transfer to a mixing bowl, stir in the sweetener and leave to cool.

● Stir the yogurt into the cooled apple purée. Beat the egg white in a clean bowl until it holds soft peaks and then fold it into the apple mixture using a metal spoon. Divide between four dessert dishes, cover with clingfilm and chill for 1 hour. Top the apple snow with the sliced apple before serving.

Top tip

When beating egg whites always start your mixer on a low speed then gradually increase the speed once they are frothy. This creates many small bubbles rather than fewer large ones, giving a more stable structure, which is especially important when making meringue mixture.

Mango and raspberry smoothie

If you're struggling to find ways to eat all of your 5 a day fruit and vegetable portions, a homemade smoothie is an easy way to boost your intake, and it tastes fabulous too.

Using whole fruits in a smoothie means that you get all the healthy fibre, so it's better for you than fruit juice.

4 POINTS values per recipe takes 5 minutes. Serves 2. Calories per serving 148. Freeze ✗

4 large ice cubes
150 ml (5 fl oz) skimmed milk
1 ripe medium mango, peeled, stoned and chopped roughly
1 ripe medium banana, chopped roughly
100 g (3½ oz) frozen raspberries
juice of ½ lemon

● Place the first five ingredients listed in a liquidiser and blend until smooth, and then add lemon juice to taste.
● Divide between two tall glasses, add drinking straws and serve immediately.

Top tip

To prepare a mango, start by removing the skin with a vegetable peeler. Mangoes have a large flat stone in the middle, so slice down each side of the stone with a knife to remove most of the flesh, then cut away any mango still attached around the stone.